SOCCER SOURCE

PLAY LIKE A PRO

SOCCER SKILLS AND DRILLS

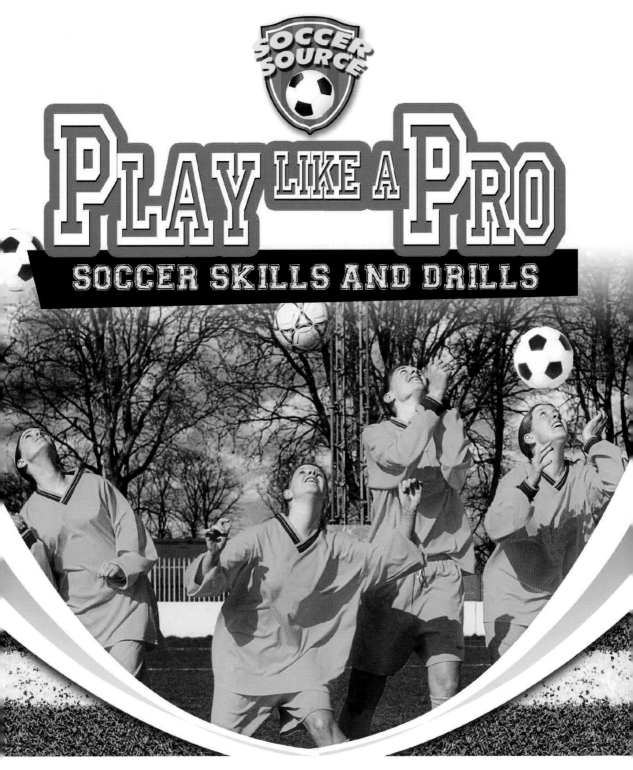

Sarah Dann

CRABTREE
Publishing Company
www.crabtreebooks.com

SOCCER SOURCE

Author
Sarah Dann

Publishing plan research and development
Kelly McNiven

Editors
Rachel Stuckey, Crystal Sikkens

Proofreader and indexer
Natalie Hyde

Photo research
Melissa McClellan

Design
Tibor Choleva

Prepress technician
Margaret Amy Salter

Print and production coordinator
Margaret Amy Salter

Consultant
Sonja Cori Missio, International soccer correspondent, featured in The Guardian, Forza Italian Football, and Soccer Newsday

Illustrations
Trevor Morgan: page 6–7

Photographs
Alamy: © Stuart Kelly (p 20); © PCN Photography (p 21 right); © Offside Sports Photography(23 bottom)
© T. Choleva (p 8)
© Marc Crabtree (p 15 bottom)
dreamstime.com: © Amy S. Myers (p 7); © Photographerlondon (17 top)
Zumapress.com/Keystone Press: © DPA (p 13 bottom);
© Molly Klager (p 14, 16, 21 left, 24)
© Melissa McClellan (p 17 bottom, 19 top)
Shutterstock.com: © ollyy (cover); © muzsy (p 3, p 25 bottom); © arindambanerjee (p 4); © Natursports (p 5, 6–7 bottom, 11 right, 20–21 top, 25 middle, 28–29 top & bottom, p 30); © Pavel L Photo and Video (6–7 top; 14–15 top, 7 bottom); © Aptyp_koK (p 9 left, right); © CLS Design (p 10); © Olga Dmitrieva (11 left); © Larry St. Pierre (13 top); © Amy Myers (p 15 top); © Maxisport (p 18); © Gyuszko-Photo (p 19 bottom); © katatonia82 (20–21 Bottom); © Photo Works (p 23 top); © Matt Trommer (25 top); © Cornelius O'Donoghue (p 26); © Yiannis Kourtoglou (p 27 top); © Michael Chamberlin (p 29 left); © Africa Studio (p 29 right)
ThinkStock: © Digital Vision (titlepage); © Brand X Pictures (p 6); FogStock (p 9 middle); © Jupiterimages (p 12); moodboard (p 22); Robert J. Beyers II (p 27 bottom); Purestock (p 28)

Created for Crabtree Publishing by BlueApple*Works*

Cover: A soccer player kicks the ball
Title page: Girls soccer team practice heading the ball

Library and Archives Canada Cataloguing in Publication

Dann, Sarah, 1970-, author
    Play like a pro : soccer skills and drills / Sarah Dann.

(Soccer source)
Includes index.
Issued in print and electronic formats.
ISBN 978-0-7787-0241-2 (bound).--ISBN 978-0-7787-0250-4 (pbk.).--
ISBN 978-1-4271-9431-2 (pdf).--ISBN 978-1-4271-9427-5 (html)

    1. Soccer--Training--Juvenile literature. I. Title.

GV943.9.T7D35 2013   j796.334   C2013-905781-1
                                              C2013-905782-X

Library of Congress Cataloging-in-Publication Data

Dann, Sarah, 1970-
  Play like a pro : soccer skills and drills / Sarah Dann.
       pages cm. -- (Soccer source)
  Includes index.
  ISBN 978-0-7787-0241-2 (reinforced library binding : alk. paper) -- ISBN 978-0-7787-0250-4 (pbk. : alk. paper) -- ISBN 978-1-4271-9431-2 (electronic pdf : alk. paper) -- ISBN 978-1-4271-9427-5 (electronic html : alk. paper)
  1. Soccer--Training--Juvenile literature. I. Title.

GV943.9.T7D36 2013
796.33407'7--dc23

2013033225

Crabtree Publishing Company

www.crabtreebooks.com   1-800-387-7650

Printed in the U.S.A./042015/CG20150312

Published in Canada
Crabtree Publishing
616 Welland Ave.
St. Catharines, Ontario
L2M 5V6

Published in the United States
Crabtree Publishing
PMB 59051
350 Fifth Avenue, 59th Floor
New York, New York 10118

Published in the United Kingdom
Crabtree Publishing
Maritime House
Basin Road North, Hove
BN41 1WR

Published in Australia
Crabtree Publishing
3 Charles Street
Coburg North
VIC 3058

CONTENTS

Soccer Around the World	4
How Do You Play?	6
Warming Up	8
Kicking the Ball	10
Dribbling and Passing	12
Trapping the Ball	14
Heading the Ball and Throw-ins	16
Working As a Team	18
Fast Forwards	20
Midfielders	22
Defenders	24
Goalkeepers	26
Sportsmanship & Nutrition	28
Play Like a Professional	30
Learning More	31
Glossary and Index	32

SOCCER AROUND THE WORLD

Soccer is one of the world's most popular sports. It is played and celebrated all around the world by men and women in international, national, and local **leagues**. It is also widely enjoyed as a **recreational** sport. Soccer has been called "the beautiful game," "the king sport," and "the world game."

Soccer's Simplicity

One of the reasons for soccer's popularity is how simple it is to play. It can be played by anyone, and almost anywhere. All you need to play is a ball and two **goal** markers. Players who do not have a ball can **improvise** and make a ball using socks, coconuts, or even scraps of fabric tied together.

Rocks, bricks, or clothing can be used to mark each side of the net.

So Many Leagues

There are thousands of soccer leagues around the world. Most leagues fall under the **Fédération Internationale de Football Association (FIFA)** which is the international governing body for soccer. Every four years, FIFA organizes a tournament called the World Cup where the best teams from countries around the world play against one another.

All around the world, soccer fans fill stadiums to cheer on their favorite teams and players.

In many countries, soccer is referred to as "football" but, in North America, it is called soccer.

Is It Soccer or Football?

It's both! The rules of soccer were set by England's Football Association in 1863. "Association Football" spread quickly around the world. "Association" was soon shortened to "assocer" and then to simply "soccer." Now, the game is known as "football" or "soccer."

HOW DO YOU PLAY?

Soccer involves kicking a ball and passing it between teammates to try and score goals on the other team's net. Players can also handle the ball using their head, chest, and legs. However, if a players touch the ball with their hands or arms on the field a **handball** is called.

Goaltenders keep the ball from going in the net. They are allowed to only use their hands inside the penalty area. A goaltender wears special gloves to help them grip the ball and stop shots.

penalty area

net

penalty spot

goal line

touch line

The Soccer Field

A soccer field is also known as a pitch. It has lines showing the **boundaries** at the ends and sides of the field. Eleven players on each team play in different **positions**. The team with the ball **attacks** and tries to score goals. The team on defense tries to **defend** against the attack and take **possession**, or control, of the ball. Each game has two halves, and at the end of the second half, whichever team has the most goals wins! If there is no score, the game can end in a **draw**, or tie, or go to extra time, or a **penalty shoot-out**.

Players throw the ball back into play when it goes outside the side boundary lines.

center line

midfielder

goalkeeper

forward

defender

There is no standard size for a soccer pitch. The longer lines along the side are called **touch lines**. The shorter lines on the ends are called **goal lines**. A **center line** in the middle divides the field in half.

WARMING UP

Soccer is a physically demanding sport which requires players to run for most of the game. Before playing, jog around the field to warm up your muscles. Once you are warm, it is important to stretch your whole body, including your neck, arms, and legs.

To stretch your hamstring muscles, sit with one leg straight out in front and point your toes upward. Bring your other foot toward your knee and reach toward your toes with your hands.

To do a lunge, bend one knee at a time, and lean over that knee to stretch your other leg. Lunges can be done to the side or going forward.

Practicing with the Ball

Ball control is an important skill to learn when you play soccer. To practice, you can run and kick the ball ahead of yourself, or you can kick the ball against a wall. You can also learn ball control by passing the ball with your friends or teammates. Start close together. Once you are able to pass the ball with **accuracy**, you can move further apart to make it harder.

*When you **juggle** a soccer ball, you keep the ball in the air by bouncing it off your feet, head, chest, and legs. This is a great skill to improve ball control and **coordination**.*

KICKING THE BALL

In a soccer game, the ball is almost always on the move. To score goals you need to learn to kick a moving ball accurately. Move toward the ball—don't wait for it to come to you. When you get close, pull your leg back and kick the ball with the inside of your foot.

Aim and Accuracy

If you kick with your right foot, approach the ball from the left and if you kick with your left foot, approach from the right. Line up your non-kicking foot with your target and the ball will go in the direction you want.

Kicking is an important skill to master to be a soccer superstar. Strong kicks can score goals and make great passes!

Against the Wall

Kicking the ball against a wall helps you practice handling the ball on the move. If you put targets on the wall, you can also practice your aim by trying to hit them.

Take time to learn how the ball moves when you kick it with different parts of your foot.

Try not to kick with your toes. Kicking with the side of your foot gives you better control with the ball.

Superstar Kicker

Argentina's Lionel Messi is considered one of the world's best soccer players. Although he is small, his aggressive play and accurate kicking have made him a leading goal scorer around the world.

In 2012, Messi made Champions League history by becoming the first player to score five goals in one match.

11

DRIBBLING AND PASSING

Moving the ball up the field with small kicks is called **dribbling**. Dribbling only requires a light touch so that the ball doesn't move too far ahead of the player. With light, accurate kicks, players can dribble the ball around their opponents.

Practice, Practice, Practice!

You can practice dribbling by setting markers in a row a few feet apart. Practice moving in between the markers while you are dribbling the ball. You can also practice with friends by taking turns running with the ball and trying to take the ball away from each other.

Dribble down the row, moving around each marker as quickly as you can without losing control of the ball.

Passing the Ball

Often it is easier to pass the ball to a teammate than to dribble the ball around players from the opposite team. Passing the ball accurately takes a lot of practice. You need to be able to move the ball in all directions at various distances.

Passing is an important skill to master.

Passing Practice

A fun way to practice passing is to stand with a group of players in a circle Take turns passing the ball to other players at different spots in the circle. To make it harder, a player in the middle of the circle can try to block the passes.

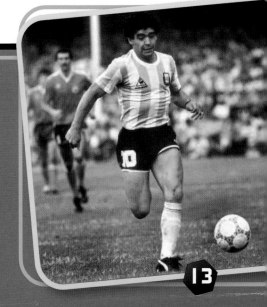

Passing Pro

Diego Maradona played soccer for Argentina until 1997. He was known not only as a top goal scorer but also for his passing skills, which often set other players up to score goals.

During his time with the Argentina national team, Maradona scored 34 goals.

13

TRAPPING THE BALL

To get control of the ball, you often need to stop it before you can kick it. This is called **trapping**. You can use your feet to stop it from rolling. However, when the ball is bouncing higher than your feet, you need to be able to stop it without using your hands. Trapping is one of the skills that makes soccer into a full body game.

Practicing Trapping

The best way to practice trapping is to have another player throw the ball to you at different heights so you can use your feet, legs, and chest to control the ball. To make this more difficult, the other player can also gently kick the ball toward you at different heights.

Many times during a game, you will need to get control of a ball that is traveling through the air or moving quickly along the ground.

Using Your Chest

Sometimes the ball comes toward you as high as your chest. Because you cannot touch the ball with your hands or arms, move them out of the way to stop the ball with your chest.

Stopping the ball with your chest will cause it to drop to the ground.

Using Your Thighs

If the ball comes in around waist level, use your knee or inner thigh to cushion the ball and let it drop to your feet.

Whichever part of your body you use as a trap, such as your foot, chest, or leg, make sure it is relaxed. If your body is stiff, the ball will bounce away from you.

HEADING THE BALL AND THROW-INS

One of the most spectacular ways to hit the ball in soccer is with your head. You are can pass the ball to another player this way or even score a goal!

Making it Work

To successfully head the ball you need to watch it carefully. You want to make contact with it just above your forehead, at your hairline. This spot allows you to direct the ball by stepping into it as you hit the ball. Bend your knees slightly and just as you hit the ball, straighten them so you can send the ball in the direction you are facing.

Players typically head the ball when it is coming toward them high in the air.

Throw-ins

Throw-ins are the one time in soccer when you are allowed to use your hands. However, throw-ins only happen when the ball has rolled out of bounds along the sides of the field. When this happens a player stands out of bounds and picks up the ball to throw it back on to the field.

Players try to throw the ball to someone on their own team and the other team tries to gain possession of it.

How to Throw-in

Throw-ins are thrown over head. The player picks up the ball in both hands and lifts it up over their head. They pull both arms back and throw the ball. The player tries to throw the ball to a teammate who is open to receive the ball.

You cannot step over the sideline when you are doing a throw-in.

WORKING AS A TEAM

While each player can work on his or her individual skills, in soccer, the team has to work together to succeed. Eleven players make up each team. There are four forwards, three midfielders, three defenders, and one goalie. Together, each team tries to score goals and keep the other team from scoring goals.

The Referee

A referee is in charge of making sure all players follow the rules. The referee follows the ball up and down the field and blows a whistle when the play needs to stop or start. Two assistants watch the lines and when the ball is kicked out of bounds, they show where exactly the ball went out so it can be thrown back in.

Most referees wear either yellow or black, but the colors and styles vary according to individual associations.

Out of Bounds in the Ends

If the ball is kicked out past the end line by the opposite team, the goalie kicks it back in. If the ball is kicked out by the goalie's own team, the opposing team gets to kick the ball in from the corner of the field on the same side of the net the ball went out on. This is called a **corner kick**.

A corner kick is taken from one of four corner circles.

Teamwork

All players work together to move the ball up the field so they can shoot on the other team's net. When players have the ball they are on **offense**. When they don't have the ball they are on **defense**.

When a team is on the offensive, all players must work together to keep the other team from gaining possession of

FAST FORWARDS

There are four forwards on the field. These players line up along the middle line on the field to start the game. The two in the center of the field are called strikers. One of these players starts the game by kicking the ball. The other two forwards on either side of the field are the left and right wingers.

Center Kick

A **center kick** begins play. Center kicks happen at the beginning of the game, after the half, and after a goal is scored. The ball is placed on the center line in the middle of the center circle. The offensive forward kicks the ball to one of their teammates, making sure the ball crosses the line into the defensive team's end.

The defensive team cannot come into the center circle until the ball has been kicked.

Speed and Scoring

Forwards tend to be some of the fastest players on the team. They need to be able to run around the other teams' players to get into position to score goals. Forwards tend to score most of a team's goals because they are placed closest to the other team's net. They need to be accurate kickers so that when they get the chance to shoot, they are more likely to score.

Forwards have to know how to kick the ball so it travels under, around, or over the other defenders and the goalie.

Superstar Forward

Mia Hamm is considered one of the best female soccer players of all time. Amongst other things, Hamm, a forward, held the record for the most goals ever scored by a soccer player, male or female, until 2013.

At 15, Mia was the youngest player to ever play for the U.S. women's national soccer team.

21

Midfielders stand between the forwards and the defenders. There are three of them—center, left wing, and right wing. The midfielders set up many of the plays since they move the ball from the defenders to the forwards. They need to have a good idea of where all their other teammates are on the field so they know where to pass the ball when they receive it.

Offense and Defense

Midfielders have to be ready to play both offense and defense. When their team has the ball they are often

attacking and trying to pass to open forwards. When the other team has the ball they try to take the ball away from the opposite players before they can reach the defenders or shoot on the net.

Midfielders do a lot of running since they are constantly moving up and down the field to get into position with the ball. They need to be very fit.

Ball Handling

Midfielders need to be calm under pressure. They most often move the ball with an opposite player guarding them closely so they need to be able to dribble and pass without losing the ball. When they do break through the other team's defense, midfielders sometimes get the chance to score. They need to be able to shoot accurately on the net.

Midfielders tend to take most of the corner kicks for their team.

Superstar Midfielder

David Beckham was an English midfielder who played professional soccer all over the world and retired in 2013. He had a great talent for the corner kick because he could arc the ball around opposing players. He even scored a few goals from the corner. It's often said that no one can *"bend it like Beckham."*

DEFENDERS

Defenders are also known as "full backs." Typically, there are three defenders on the field at one time—centre, left, and right. Defenders are the last players on the field before the goalie and the net. Their job is to keep the ball from being shot at the net. They carefully watch the other teams forwards and midfielders, guarding them and blocking the ball if it is shot at the net.

Strategic positioning

Defenders can either be directly beside an attacking player, or in between the attacking player and the net. Either way, the aim is to take the ball away from the shooter or block a kicked ball before it can reach the net.

Defending the net often requires defenders to head the ball.

Superstar Defender

Sergio Ramos is one of the world's top defenders. He plays for Real Madrid and the Spanish national team, which won the World Cup in 2010. He is a great defensive player, but is also talented at scoring goals, which makes him somewhat unique in this position.

Sergio Ramos scores a headed goal during a soccer game in Madrid, Spain.

Moving the Ball

Defenders sometimes kick the ball far up the field to set up plays in cases when they receive the ball without pressure from the other team. This can happen when an opposing player loses control of the ball or when a midfielder from the defender's team passes the ball back.

Whenever possible, if a full back gets the ball away from an offensive player, they then try to pass the ball to a member of their own team.

GOALKEEPERS

The goalkeeper's main role is to keep the ball out of the net. After the ball is saved, goalkeepers put the ball back in play by passing it to a teammate. The goalie is the only player on the field who can use their hands and arms to catch or block the ball.

Kicking the Ball

When the goalie is putting the ball back in play they can throw it or roll it to another player. More commonly, the goalie kicks the ball. They can take three steps before dropping the ball on to their foot and kicking it up the field. This is called **punting** and when done properly it passes the ball to an open player, even if they are far up the field.

Goalies can only use their hands within their goalie box and inside the penalty kick area on the field.

Cutting the Angle

When under attack, goalies often come out of their net to cut the angle of the approaching player. This means the goalie comes closer to the player leaving them less room to shoot on the net. The net is high and wide so goalies need to have a good idea of where the goal posts are behind them to be able to successfully stop a shot. Sometimes a goalie jumps up and punches the ball away from the net.

Great Soccer Goalie

Gianluigi Buffon is regarded as the world's best goalkeeper. He has played for over 15 years in Italy and is the highest paid goalkeeper in the world.

Gianluigi Buffon is nicknamed "Superman" and is widely known for his "outstanding shot-stopping."

*(left) Ideally the goalie stays on their feet when making a save. It makes it harder to stop a **rebound** if the goalie has fallen on the first shot.*

27

SPORTSMANSHIP & NUTRITION

With so many players on your own team and other players on the field, one of the most important things in soccer is to show good sportsmanship. Not only is it important to get along well with your own team, it is also important to be respectful of the other team.

Your Own Team

Good sportsmanship on your own team means making sure that you set other players up to succeed and don't just try to take all the glory for yourself. Your team will play better if you have everyone's success in mind.

The soccer field is too big to tackle alone. Being a team player makes the game more fun for everyone.

Your Opponents

Soccer players are very close together on the field. Being respectful of other players, means making sure others do not get hurt as you play the game. Kicking can injure other players if you are not careful. Although it is important to get the ball, it is also important to do your best to make sure no one else gets hurt while you do so.

Shaking hands with the opposing team players after the game shows good sportsmanship.

Nutrition

To make sure you have success on the field you need to stay fit. Eating properly off the field and drinking a lot of water during games are important. You can stay fit by staying away from sugary foods and drinks.

Drinks made with fruits and vegetables are a healthy snack for off the field.

PLAY LIKE A PROFESSIONAL

For those of you who really love soccer, sign up to play in a local league or on your school soccer team. You can even just play with your friends! Many of the best players in the world started playing at a very young age. Soccer players are lucky because there are so many organized leagues across the U.S. and around the world. It makes it easier to keep playing as you get older and better at the game.

Watching Soccer

You can watch soccer games played locally or at a national level. Watching professionals can give you a good sense of how the game is played at the highest levels around the world. This could be you one day. Just keep playing, stay fit, and don't give up!

Players and fans around the world make soccer one of the most widely watched sports in the world. Almost every country has its own league and its own national team.

LEARNING MORE

Books

Crisfield, Deborah W. *The Everything Kids' Soccer Book: Rules, techniques and more about your favorite sport!* F-W Media, Inc. 2009.

Gifford, Clive. *Soccer Skills.* Kingfisher. 2005.

Goin, Kenn. *Soccer for Fun!* Compass Point Books, 2003.

FIFA World Cup

Learn all about the biggest tournament in the world—the FIFA World Cup. Coming up in 2014, the FIFA World Cup brings together the top teams in the world with qualifying games happening continuously in the off years.

www.fifa.com/worldcup/

U.S Soccer Teams

Find out all about the U.S. Men and Women's Soccer Teams including team information for all age groups, tournament details and schedules, and team blogs including a youth team blog.

www.ussoccer.com

Soccer Tips

For tips about playing soccer, there are a lot of videos available on You Tube and online. This site gives quite a bit of information to help you understand soccer plays and strategies as well as conditioning. The Soccer Drills Directory gives suggestions for drills by age group so make sure you find ones that suit your age.

www.soccer-training-info.com

GLOSSARY

Note: Some boldfaced words are defined where they appear in the book.

accuracy Being careful and precise

attacks Trying to score or create goal-scoring opportunities

boundaries Lines that make up the outer limits of a space like a field

center kick A kick taken from the center circle to start the game, the half, or after a goal

citizens People who live in a state or country

coordination Making things happen together

corner kick A kick taken from the corner of the field by an attacking player when a defending player kicks the ball out of bounds beside their net

defend Trying to keep the other team from scoring

defense Refers to the team without the ball who is defending

goal The space into which a player shoots the ball to score

improvise Making something from materials not intended for that purpose

leagues An organized group of teams who compete against each other

offense Refers to the team with the ball who is on the attack

penalty shoot-out Shots taken on net to settle a tie game

positions Where each person plays

possession When a player or team has the ball

punting Kicking the ball after you drop it from your hands

rebound When the goalie saves the ball but it bounces back into play and is kicked at the net again

recreational Playing for fun but not in an organized league

INDEX

attack 7, 22, 24
Beckham, David 23
Buffon, Gianluigi 27
defending 7, 19, 20, 21, 22, 24, 25
dribbling 12, 23
goaltenders 6, 18, 26, 27
Hamm, Mia 21
handball 6
Maradona, Diego 13
Messi, Lionel 11
punting 26
Ramos, Sergio 25
referee 18
trapping 14, 15